My Mirrored Soul and Personal Spiritual Journey

Table of Contents

Introduction - Family Morals and Values

Growing up in a Christian environment, I was taught at a very young age how to worship and serve God, along with treating people with respect, learning mannerisms, and understanding how to behave in front of adults as a small child. As a child, one tends to look up to the dominant figures in their life, such as parents, grandparents, aunts, uncles, and family members, considering them as superheroes. These individuals are perceived as superheroes because they cater to all your needs, and as a child, you have yet to learn how to manage things on your own, making their actions extraordinary in the eyes of a child. Throughout childhood, the primary desire is to experience nurturing love from parents, guardians, or close family members, whether consciously acknowledged or not.

As I grew older and interacted with children my age, as well as some younger, I began to realize that not all families were similar to mine. Some kids had lost their parents at an early age, never knew them, or came from homes where family units were separated due to inadequate care, leading to placement in foster care. Witnessing the brokenness of some individuals on my life path was heartbreaking, and it dawned on me that there were disparities in the world in terms of how life was lived, as well as variances within myself.

I always felt distinct from my immediate family, unable to pinpoint the reason. It's plausible that my unique perspective stemmed from being the only water sign in my household, surrounded by earth signs. Strange occurrences in my childhood and an innate intuition were memorable aspects. I distinctly recall being unusually afraid of one of my grade school teachers, frequently crying in her class without understanding the intensity of my emotions. At seven or eight years old, my comprehension of emotions was limited. However, I recognized an instinctive need to pray, an unusual behavior for a child my age. I sought solace in prayer during recess, talking out loud to God, sensing a protective presence shielding me from unfavorable circumstances.

As I matured, I transitioned to quiet prayers, influenced by saying them aloud at home before bedtime until my sister requested me to do so quietly. Reflecting on my past, I still struggle to explain occurrences between ages seven and nine, a period when I should have been resting. I developed a pattern of staying awake until my dad returned home from work, then sleeping throughout the morning, waking up well past noon. This routine persisted for an extended period.

There were moments when I witnessed certain occurrences that made it difficult for me to sleep through the night, even when he was at home. I couldn't articulate this to my parents because, in their perspective, it didn't exist. Nevertheless, peculiar incidents occurred while I was asleep. I distinctly recall this particular day because it remains a mystery to me. I was sleeping at the top of my bed, yet upon waking up, I found myself at the foot of my bed with no clothes on, as if I had been in a physical altercation. The sensation was as if my dream had materialized right before me. Though still highly inexplicable, the experience was undeniably real.

Numerous events from my childhood played a pivotal role in shaping the person I am today. However, the most significant influence was the transmission of morals and values from my parents and grandparents. Additionally, I gained valuable guidance, wisdom, and knowledge from various sources, including family, friends, church members, and the community.

Chapter One - Having the Desire
For the One

I developed a desire for "the one" at a very young age. Somehow, I always found myself drawn to younger individuals, and they, in turn, were drawn to me. My initial crush occurred in second grade, where I recall him being in the first grade. Our paths crossed in aftercare, and that's how I got to know him. He wasn't the type of person most would approach at first glance, but his constant smile and wit appealed to me greatly. Unfortunately, I had to change schools by my third grade year due to living near a different one, preventing me from expressing my feelings. This left me feeling crushed. Despite experiencing various crushes, none matched the intensity of meeting "the one."

Before encountering my true life partner, I navigated a toxic relationship. At that point, I lacked a clear understanding of my self-worth, as I was just beginning my journey and had yet to comprehend what a healthy relationship entailed. My father had shared his perspective on how a marriage should be, leaving me without a solid grasp of the distinction between a marriage and a relationship until later in life. I devoted myself wholeheartedly to my partner, unaware that I was overgiving, and received little reciprocation. Although it took time to realize, that relationship eventually came to an end.

While working, I met someone interested in dating me. Despite initially expressing that I wasn't ready, his vibrant and exciting energy convinced me to give it another try with someone who genuinely wanted to be with me. Although we were different, we shared a deep love, yet frequently clashed. Three years into our relationship, he proposed, and we were married on Valentine's Day. Despite our love, numerous questions plagued my thoughts as we prepared to walk down the aisle. Intuition gnawed at me, but I proceeded, only to realize it didn't unfold as I had anticipated.

On the day of our marriage, a voice within me whispered, "You weren't supposed to marry him." It felt as if my true life partner was communicating that they were still out there. This marked the turning point when my yearning for "the one" intensified. As the years unfolded within my marriage, my desire for that elusive life partner remained steadfast.

As I attempted to sustain the relationship, I found that with increasing age and maturity, I discovered a lack of fulfillment. It became evident that despite my efforts to contribute as I had done in the past, my own needs were not being met. The dissatisfaction stemmed from my spouse's discontent with both their life and career. Though I cared enough to step away once he became self-sufficient, the marriage no longer resonated with my true self, and I found myself disliking the person I had become. Our mutual learning experience revealed that a successful marriage demanded more than just love. Consequently, we made the difficult decision to part ways, yet we share the responsibility of raising our child.

Ironically, the very thing I vowed not to do, I eventually succumbed to – seeking a divorce. During this period, fate intervened, and I encountered "the one" once again, coincidentally within the same workplace. Going about my business, I noticed new faces on the shift. As I glanced down the aisle, I unexpectedly identified the person as "the one." Initially unaware of his significance, our eyes met as he walked past my area. In that moment, a voice within me affirmed, "that's him," leading me to deny the possibility. Yet, the voice persisted, and as anticipated, he approached. Upon hearing his voice, I not only recognized it, but he, too, recognized me.

Realizing the profound connection, I acknowledged the impossibility of our acquaintance, given his seven-year juniority. However, it became evident that the recognition was mutual. A powerful force seemed to underlie our connection. Intrigued, I observed commonalities in our habits, such as using the same washing powder and soap, even without verbal discussion. This prompted a desire to delve deeper into the mysterious connection we shared.

Chapter Two - Meeting the One

After encountering "the one," my desire to delve deeper into our connection intensified. I had never encountered someone whose personality mirrored mine so closely yet differed in its own unique way. The connection we shared was remarkably intense, unlike any other I had experienced before. Meeting "the one" defied conventional expectations; it wasn't a sensation most people associate with such encounters.

When our eyes met, an inner certainty enveloped me. I seldom engage in eye contact the way we did, but in that moment, I recognized the significance of this person in my life. It wasn't a case of love at first sight; rather, it felt like a reunion, a sense of "I missed you." When he greeted me with a playful "hello mean lady," I instantly recognized his voice. Despite a seven-year age difference and divergent interests, our thoughts resonated in a peculiarly similar manner.

We evolved into close friends, yet the intense bond I felt with him puzzled me. It surpassed any connection I had experienced with my spouse or family. Every interaction at work filled me with excitement, making the prospect of going to work a joy. Even those around me noticed my newfound happiness, an emotion I had unwittingly displayed. It felt akin to being in my own company, yet through someone else.

As he was temporarily hired for construction, our interactions dwindled when he changed shifts. However, the time we spent together remained invaluable. Weeks and months passed without seeing him, prompting me to question God about his whereabouts. Despite God's assurance that he was the one, I experienced a sense of sadness and longing. I fervently prayed that if he truly was the one, he would return to my life.

Lacking any means of contact, both he and I moved on with our lives. I hoped to encounter him again but remained uncertain. During a Christmas shopping excursion with my sister, my wish came true – I saw him back at work.

I realized at that moment that my feelings for him were remarkably strong when I entered the bathroom to ensure that my hair and face were in order before approaching him. Seeing him filled me with immense joy, and I couldn't contain my smile, nor could he. From that point on, I knew I loved him. However, in our world, it's uncommon to express such feelings without being in a committed relationship. Additionally, one often hesitates to confess love first, wanting to gauge whether the other person reciprocates. I kept my feelings to myself, wanting to be certain of their authenticity.

The love I feel for this man is unlike any other; it's a rarity. Normally, I am not inclined towards being overly emotional, but with him, I find myself melting like butter. I can only share my personal experience of encountering 'the one,' and it varies for everyone. Some may experience love at first sight, while others may need time to get to know someone better. Depending on your emotional state when you meet that special person, you might not immediately recognize them, especially if you've recently faced heartache and closed yourself off. The true essence of love becomes most apparent when you're open to receiving and giving it.

Chapter Three - Head over Heels in Love

Before I knew it, I found myself head over heels in love—an emotion entirely unfamiliar to me. In my previous relationships, which were admittedly scarce, initial happiness would often give way to the harsh reality that the connection was either a toxic karmic bond, a lesson I needed to glean from the person, or a signal for personal change. Nevertheless, these earlier connections felt more akin to infatuations or intense likings; love, in the truest sense, had eluded me.

I loved those individuals, as I do everyone, but true love, the kind that resonates with a sense of home and familiarity, had remained elusive. Being head over heels, as I understood it, seemed more like a trope from television, prompting occasional doubts about the authenticity of my emotions. There were instances when I consciously withdrew my energy, questioning the veracity of what I felt.

In his presence, I would smile and laugh effortlessly, even when nothing particularly amusing was happening. Those around us would sometimes express curiosity about my seemingly inexplicable laughter. My joy, however, emanated from a profound sense of happiness. I vividly recall a moment when we had planned to meet early in the morning, and he called to inform me of an unexpected commitment with his father that day. The disappointment was profound, akin to a bereavement. I couldn't drive home; my tears flowed uncontrollably.

In that poignant moment, I realized the intensity of this newfound love. If such a brief encounter could evoke such a profound emotional response, I grappled with the fear of how I would navigate this unfamiliar terrain. The prospect of our connection either faltering or progressing to a deeper level became a source of both anticipation and trepidation.

At that moment, I perceived it as a viable prospect, primarily because, in my mind, I failed to discern any reason why it wouldn't work. The foundation was solid with our strong camaraderie and profound care for each other. Additionally, the sheer enjoyment we derived from each other's company bolstered my optimism. Experiencing such a robust friendship and profound affection for an individual was a rarity for me, particularly with my mirrored soul. Naturally, I harbored a desire to explore the potential trajectory of this connection. However, a lingering uncertainty about the nature of our bond persisted in the recesses of my mind. Despite this, I was certain that this was precisely where I wanted to be.

Being head over heels, for me, meant contemplating a person, yearning to exchange greetings, and relishing their presence. During that period, this held significant weight for me. If an individual failed to capture my attention with intelligence or articulate speech, I tended not to dwell on them. Even as a teenager, I dismissed those who appeared too old for my class, as I perceived it as indicative of a lack of commitment to self-improvement and academic excellence—qualities I sought for myself.

My venture into serious dating commenced later than most, driven by a profound belief that I had yet to encounter someone capable of sustaining my interest for an extended duration. That is, until now.

Chapter Four - The Dream Come True Love Feeling

This was the kind of love I had always desired but doubted its existence until it materialized. It still seemed surreal to me, given what I had observed and heard from others regarding their connections. I refrained from discussing my dream come true love with others because many around me were grappling with issues in their connections. I was wary of their influences affecting my perception of what a connection should be. What I experienced was markedly different from what others professed.

I found myself in a relationship where my partner genuinely cared about my well-being, ensuring I rested, inquiring about my day, and expressing concern for my eating habits—elements often overlooked in interpersonal connections. Many connections I had before my mirrored soul connection were characterized by self-serving motives, with the focus on what I could do for them to attain happiness. Conversely, I derived little or no benefit from these connections, and my needs were often disregarded.

In retrospect, those prior connections served as valuable life lessons for me. The truth is, the dream come true feeling is somewhat illusory at the inception of a mirrored soul connection. It only transforms into reality after investing effort in personal growth. However, one enters such a spiritual connection without being aware of this fact. Some mirrored soul connections effortlessly endure, while others demand significant effort. Undertaking such a challenging journey requires an old soul.

The authenticity of true love is undeniable, but the journey to unravel its depths necessitates substantial effort. It takes a genuine person to honestly express their emotions. I soon realized that my previous connections were vastly different from the one I courageously embraced. The intensity of the new connection surpassed the mere warm-up of the prior ones. Unprepared for what unfolded next, I remained open to the experience, driven by the pursuit of love, true love.

For me, true love holds paramount importance in a connection. I have often heard people express the sentiment that they prioritize financial security above love in a relationship. However, for me, love must be the foundation, as I believe that everything else falls into place naturally when fueled by genuine affection.

If one seeks a partner solely for the purpose of being taken care of and ensuring their material needs are met, it seems to resemble the role of a parent rather than that of a lover, in my opinion. The responsibility for such care typically lies with fathers, mothers, parents, or guardians until individuals reach an age where they can provide for themselves.

At times, we construct a life based on societal expectations, assuming that everyone should follow a similar path. Yet, the beauty of life lies in our diversity— our distinct interests, preferences, and tastes that we can share with others. Not all of us are alike or desire the same things, and this diversity is what makes life rich and fascinating.

While the prospect of everyone engaging in identical pursuits may seem monotonous to me, true love, in my perspective, is characterized by its purity, naturalness, and the ease with which it flows when authentic. Attempting to force compatibility can disrupt this natural flow and manipulating it may lead to eventual disconnection.

Connecting with your true love does not imply the absence of challenges, but the ability to resolve them swiftly arises from effective communication with someone you genuinely love and cherish. If, despite finding someone you believe to be "the one," you encounter persistent issues that resist resolution, it may indicate internal challenges requiring individual attention.

Our preconceived notions about how love should unfold can sometimes hinder our ability to recognize and embrace it. However, something truly meant for you is unlikely to be missed.

Chapter Five - The Overwhelming Feeling of Insecurity with greater Intensity

The love shared between two divine individuals is incredibly intense, to say the least. There were times when we would physically shock each other, and often, I would feel lightheaded in his presence, though I'm not sure I ever told him that. I began paying more attention to things I probably wouldn't have in any other connection. When we actually started dating, I thought, "I must have forgotten how to do this after being married for twelve years," because everything seemed so different. I thought that there was more I needed to do because I would often feel a push-pull energy from my mirrored soul. That's when I truly realized that this connection wasn't going to be easy.

I began asking myself more questions than I used to about my connection with my counterpart. Is it something I am doing wrong? Am I doing too much? Am I doing enough? Why does it seem like he's running? Am I a good catch? Why would he settle for something that's least like him? These were all common questions I asked time and time again, questions I never asked myself in the past. Then I asked, "Is this the one? Why do I not have an answer to an obvious question?" And subsequently, I pondered, "Are there others who date and ask similar questions? Are these common questions to ask when dating?"

I don't recall being so absorbed in my thoughts, still oblivious to the true nature of this journey and its significance in terms of personal growth and learning. Over time, our connection shifted from attraction to repulsion, blurring the line between love and hate. It was a unique kind of love, the type you feel for someone whose essence and capabilities you understand, even if not always visibly demonstrated. It's an unconditional love, akin to how we love ourselves.

In such a profound connection, overanalysis and overthinking become prevalent. There are moments when it seems like your partner has it all together, leaving you questioning why they're drawn to you. These were some of the challenges we confronted. The intensity of our relationship surpassed any I had experienced before, requiring moments of solitude to realign due to the overwhelming energy.

As we weren't consistently in sync, the intensity soared. During these periods, we likely spent more time apart than together because being in the challenging energy was overwhelming. Unaware of my empathic nature at the time, it became a natural response for me to distance myself from an environment that deeply affected me.

Chapter Six - The Challenge: Runner/Chaser

I didn't realize such dynamics existed in a connection until I encountered my mirrored soul. We alternated roles as the runner and the chaser, a reflection of our willingness to address any issues that arose. Looking back, this pattern indicated that he was committed to resolving the challenges we faced. I would run, thinking he wasn't serious; then he would run, harboring similar doubts. There were times when it felt like I was navigating the connection alone for extended periods, only to find him reappear, and we'd be content again.

During moments of confusion, I turned to prayer, seeking answers about the nature of our connection and whether I was truly in one. The lack of direct communication from my mirrored soul left me questioning. At that time, fear likely played a role, as I was adamant about not losing the person I genuinely loved, and perhaps our fears mirrored each other.

I couldn't fathom why two souls desiring the same thing struggled to communicate. It felt like something essential was left unsaid, lingering in the unspoken realm. Though I still didn't fully grasp the nature of our connection, I sensed a divine guidance bringing us together—no mere coincidence. Despite several small separations, the final one was markedly different. He seemed transformed, almost unrecognizable, and the mood was unfamiliar. This departure was accompanied by an attitude I had never witnessed, instilling a sense of fear. Despite the shocking behavior, I remained in love with him even as he chose to walk away without a word, a stark departure from our usual ability to talk, joke, and find joy together, even in challenging times.

We were entirely out of sync, repelling each other more than drawing closer. Our energies, life paths, and vibrational frequencies were unbalanced. Perspectives on how people connect and the priorities for both of us were shifting, altering even the way we perceived each other.

Many may have experienced similar connections, not exclusively romantic ones but also with family and friends. There are times when you can't completely distance yourself from someone, despite the desire to do so. Yet, you sense there's a reason for their presence, even if intermittent breaks are necessary. After a cycle of pursuing and evading, exhaustion sets in, and that's precisely what happened to me. I thought, "Lord, if it's truly meant for me, it will never pass me by," and I ceased running and chasing.

Chapter Seven - The Separation, Surrendering, and Letting Go

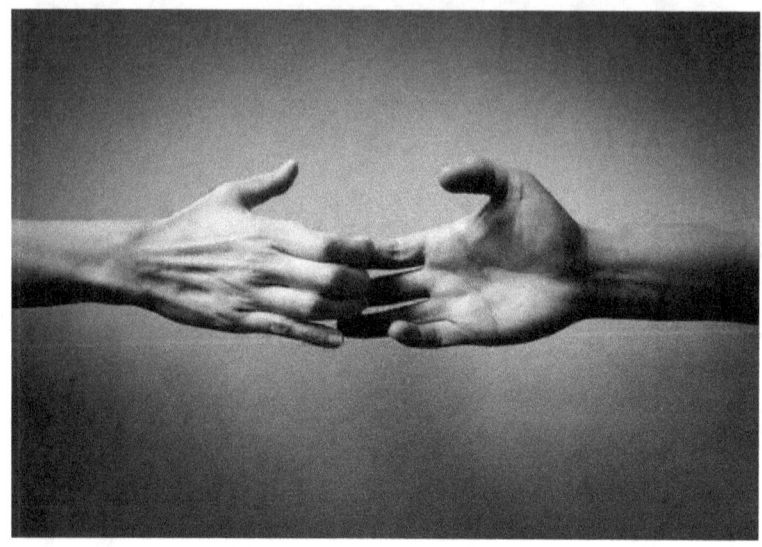

Surrendering and letting go proved to be the most challenging task I had ever faced. The difficulty stemmed from relinquishing the perceived control I thought I held and detaching myself from specific outcomes. It's common for us to envision an ideal future with the person, career, and life of our dreams. However, I needed to refrain from being overly specific, particularly regarding the person I deeply loved and cared for. While I had a vision for my life, my focus shifted to finding happiness within myself.

Spirit frequently reminded me that my mirrored soul would return in due time. I consistently expressed to Spirit that I would only receive him when he was ready. I acknowledged that persuasion or force wouldn't bring anyone back, and after numerous divine interventions,

I grasped the illusion of his absence. We would never truly part because we are one soul. Spirit advised me to live my life, have fun, and explore, assuring me that my mirrored soul was in its rightful place.

During the separation stage of this journey, I discovered the true significance of his presence. Telepathic communication persisted, revealing his remorse and profound apologies. He frequently visited me in my dreams, checking on me as I slept.

It was his way of protecting me, and there were even times when his parents and siblings conveyed messages to me in my dreams. The initial day of our separation, or the illusion of it, coincided with my birthday three years ago. I sensed it was approaching; my chest palpitated differently. I often believed that the heart murmur, initially predicted to outgrow, intensified after his birth. An echocardiogram revealed a heartbeat identical to his. As he began distancing himself months before my birthday, I physically felt it. Mistakenly interpreting it as chest pains, a hospital visit diagnosed it as separation anxiety, attributed to my daughter leaving for college. However, on my birthday, I realized the true source of anxiety.

He abruptly cut off contact, changed his number, and at that moment, Spirit assured me he would return. The separation was necessary to safeguard the connection, orchestrated by the divine. At the time, I was furious, feeling that I meant enough to him for a conversation instead of a sudden departure. When I mention Spirit intervening, he later had to explain on his behalf what had transpired.

He informed me that he wasn't prepared yet, emphasizing that there were still lessons he needed to glean from others to ready himself. Although uncertain about the duration, I placed my trust in the guidance of spirit, confident that the culmination would occur in this lifetime due to the consistent communication he maintained. I relinquished my anger, redirecting it into compassion and love, recognizing his need for support.

As an empath, I received his telepathic distress calls regarding jobs and various aspects of his life. Despite the emotional challenge, I embraced understanding and empathy because he relied on me. Declarations of love were conveyed verbally, but more profoundly felt within. While I acknowledged the difficulty of letting go and surrendering, keeping my feelings and thoughts confined solely to the realm of spirit was equally arduous. Following spiritual counsel, I refrained from discussing our union with others who might not share similar beliefs, as it was advised that such conversations could potentially delay the union. Consequently, I maintained a restrained approach, allowing God to take charge as advised.

When my mirrored soul unexpectedly distanced himself from me, it felt akin to having the rug pulled out from under me, catching me off guard. Recalling a dream from several years prior, where he lay beside me, added an extra layer of contemplation.

It began as an intimately charged dream, but within its narrative, we were unexpectedly discovered by his pastor. Before any words were exchanged, he abruptly fled, and I pursued him until we reached a critical point where he, unfortunately, ended his life before catching up to him. The intensity of the dream left me waking with a pounding heart. I instinctively kissed him, expressing relief that he was still beside me. When I recounted the dream to him, he vehemently denied any intention of such actions. Ironically, he had indeed run away, just as in the dream. However, this time, I refrained from chasing him, fully aware of the dream's outcome. I chose to let go.

Chapter Eight - The Reuniting of One

This is a phase of my journey that not everyone will reach in any lifetime, unless the necessary work is undertaken. It constitutes both the best and most challenging part, particularly if an ego death fails to transpire. I sensed that this juncture awaited me, having been forewarned that this lifetime presented the sole opportunity to connect with my mirrored soul. While the concept of choice and free will still persisted, my will aligned with God's will.

Reuniting with a mirrored soul often spans multiple lifetimes, hindered by cultural, familial, occupational, religious, age-related, or other impediments that divert individuals from their true paths of growth and transcendence. The distractions of the world frequently lead us astray, causing us to neglect our individual needs and the calls of our souls. I had to learn and train my mind to prioritize these aspects for the reunion to materialize. Divine intervention occurred when God instructed me to let his team work behind the scenes on my behalf, urging me to embrace life and share love with all I hold dear.

Spirit cautioned me to be flexible and make adjustments when the anticipated meeting took place, as it wouldn't unfold as expected. I anticipated an unconventional reunion, as my mirrored soul hadn't explicitly revealed the purpose of their return to me. Spirit, however, conveyed this information. Any messages from spirit regarding my mirrored soul's return would only manifest if he was genuinely prepared to come back.

When I eventually let go of my yearning for a reunion and embraced living my life, I started noticing angel numbers and his initials appearing everywhere. On that particular day, I vocalized my realization, saying, "Today is the day my mirrored soul will reach out." It was a moment I could feel, and remarkably, he emailed me that very day after two years of silence.

The most perplexing aspect of his silence was that he never communicated as much with me until the separation. Our telepathic connection was an incredibly potent force. Through this silent communication channel, he shared his feelings, thoughts, and experiences, aspects he was hesitant to discuss in the tangible world. In my dreams, he apologized numerous times and reassured me that he hadn't truly left. On the day he unexpectedly withdrew from my life, coincidentally my birthday, he passionately kissed me. He would appear beside me in dreams, sensing my need for his presence.

Anticipation grew as I looked forward to encountering him in the real world again, albeit with a transformed perspective. My spiritual growth had matured, allowing me to comprehend the underlying currents. It dawned on me that both of us had put in the necessary work; we were different individuals now. An ego death had taken place, and we seamlessly resumed our lives as if someone had pressed pause and then hit play. Engaging in a soul connection at such a profound level is undeniably challenging and rare, achievable only by the oldest of souls with steadfast determination. It serves as a profound teacher, revealing the core of who you are, flaws and all, through a soul identical to your own.

When you reject your soul, it reflects aspects of yourself that you dislike, leading to a natural repulsion until you address and acknowledge those inner issues. The realization dawns that you are essentially seeing yourself in another person's mirror. In a connection of mirrored souls, the profound similarity prompts introspection. If you find it challenging to be with that person, it implies a difficulty within yourself. Changes you undergo also influence them, whether consciously recognized or not.

Although my mirrored soul has returned, it marks the beginning of a new journey for both of us. Mirrored soul connections can take various forms — some remain platonic, fostering mutual learning, while others provide the closure needed for individuals to move on to a tranquil life. The nature of the connection is shaped by personal desires and needs.

In my case, surrendering and making necessary changes were crucial not only for my own growth but also to aid my mirrored soul in overcoming obstacles, the specifics of which I wasn't fully aware of. Helping myself simultaneously contributed to his well-being, given the mirrored nature of our lives. Our upbringing mirrored each other, from the number of siblings to both being the oldest, even down to experiencing chickenpox simultaneously. Despite a seven-year age gap, we shared synchronous feelings. Looking back, the reason for my heightened emotions in second grade becomes clear — the toddler stage he was in and our unspoken connection. Contracting chickenpox around ages eight or nine and two, respectively, doesn't strike me as a mere coincidence.

Chapter Nine - My Spiritual Journey and Mirrored Soul Journey

Firstly, I want to express my gratitude to God, who truly holds the helm of my life, my spiritual guides, guardian angels, ancestors, spiritual leaders, and everyone who contributed to the creation of this biography—the individuals who have crossed my path. The spiritual aspect of my journey has undoubtedly been the most challenging. Navigating through various philosophies and beliefs about spirituality makes it difficult to convey to those who have yet to experience their own spiritual journey or comprehend what it truly means to be on that path.

For months, the spirit urged me to share my journey with the world, with the hope of inspiring others to embrace change and understand the underlying reasons for the events in their lives. Our existence is governed by cycles, or as some may put it, numerous assignments. Failing to complete a cycle correctly results in its repetition, whether it pertains to love, money, family, or careers—all interconnected with love. Consider this: if you were enduring mistreatment in a love connection, would you remain in it merely to maintain the connection, or would you believe you deserve better and seek a more fulfilling connection? The same principle applies to a job or career. Staying in situations that don't serve your best interests may stem from undervaluing yourself, settling for less. However, the world offers a plethora of endless opportunities. Why limit yourself? Why not explore them? These are the questions that arise when the need for change becomes apparent.

These were questions that I found myself pondering. Society instills in us the importance of attending the best schools, consistently striving for excellence, securing top-notch jobs, only for us to discover along our journeys that the paths we've chosen may not align with our highest good. Initially promising, these paths may lose their luster, leaving us unfulfilled and discontent. These realizations unfolded both before and after my father's passing. I sensed that God was preparing me for something significant, understanding how I would cope with the loss. This preparation began well before his illness manifested, marking the initiation of my spiritual journey.

I was employed by a company that many would deem a dream job. The path to this role emerged from my dreams, and I harbored the certainty that I would eventually leave my then-current job. In a moment, likely around 2008 in the spring or summer, seated at my desk amidst a pile of work, I heard a voice in my right ear, a spiritual urging commanding me to fax my resume. Perceiving the authority in that voice, I spent the entire day faxing my resume, relinquishing my attention to the existing workload, trusting in God to guide me blindly. As the day concluded, I informed my coworker that I would be departing in October, to which she simply replied, "okay."

I received a call from my dream job, quite literally because the location and the company's name appeared to me in a dream. So, on the day of the interview, I felt relaxed, convinced I had secured the position. I commenced this job on October 6, 2008, and it was everything I had ever wanted. However, as is common in most workplaces, changes occurred. There were shifts in management, alterations in coworkers, and adjustments in staffing—changes that I too underwent.

Initially, the environment was incredibly welcoming, but gradually, it turned toxic. There were several incidents that propelled me onto my spiritual path, particularly a day when I witnessed two coworkers being bullied by management. One resigned with a week's notice and was informed that due to not providing a two-week notice, she wouldn't receive a bonus. However, bonuses were already delayed by months. The other coworker, who was close to my daughter's age, was being belittled and spoken down to as if she were not an adult. In my eyes, she was new to the workforce, still transitioning from the smaller pond to the vast ocean. This deeply affected me because I strongly believe in fair and respectful treatment, none of which was evident from the management. I remember entering the building that day feeling as if I was stepping into a fog-covered cemetery, with the worst headache I'd ever experienced.

Leaving for home, I found solace in prayer and gospel music, and it was during this time that the lyrics "He waited" from Travis Greene's song resonated deeply. It struck me as a direct message, and I found myself crying all the way home, realizing that God was waiting for me to make the necessary changes—changes I should have made long ago but had hesitated to pursue.

I left my previous job in 2018 to embark on my entrepreneurial journey, establishing my own business. However, during the process, I found myself working for another company while simultaneously building my own venture. Initially joining as a temporary employee, I consistently reassured myself that it was a temporary situation, so it didn't matter whether I became a permanent fixture. Although this company was highly coveted by most, my initial interest was not in working for them, but rather in understanding how a company could start with minimal funds and grow into a significant entity. I envisioned myself following a similar path.

Various individuals in management and some of my coworkers, at different intervals, approached me, urging me to consider a permanent position. Despite their suggestions, I always declined, maintaining that it was meant to be a temporary arrangement. However, there came a pivotal moment when a coworker from a different shift approached me in a manner that conveyed a message beyond his own words. He asked, "Have you applied for that job yet? What are you waiting for? Stop being hard-headed; you're going to get it." I sensed a spiritual authority speaking through him, compelling me to take his advice. Consequently, I applied and successfully secured the position. I recognized that this coworker was merely a vessel, a conduit for a higher force guiding my path. When I later mentioned his words to him, he denied ever saying such things, affirming that it was not his usual way of speaking. I understood, as I had previously thought, why would he be concerned about my choices?

We perform distinct roles and operate on different shifts. It dawned on me that this wasn't the first instance of spiritual communication through people. Even my ex-husband, at a seemingly random moment, conveyed a message from God, remarking on my change from speaking loudly to whispering, a fact he doesn't recall to this day. I realized that his encouragement for me to apply for the job stemmed from his foresight; they eventually phased out temporary positions, relying solely on permanent staff.

This revelation occurred during the Covid-19 pandemic, a time when the need for fewer people in confined spaces arose unexpectedly. Prior to departing my previous job at a global specimen processing lab, a field susceptible to overseas samples, I foresaw the potential risks. I distinctly recall expressing to my work neighbor, seated beside me, my reluctance to remain in a situation where unknown substances could emerge, be it from overseas or within the United States. Consequently, I chose to distance myself from that role, fortuitously avoiding the challenges posed by the processing of Covid-19 tests. Now, with a newfound understanding, I am equipped to navigate my career path strategically.

During that period, my dad suffered a stroke, and uncertainty lingered regarding the trajectory of his recovery. However, a peculiar incident occurred when my daughter and I spotted an owl outside the hospital during daylight hours. The owl, seemingly gazing directly at us, left me perplexed. Seeking understanding, I implored God for more time with my dad. Miraculously, I was granted an additional six years to spend with him. In the months leading up to his eventual passing, a profound moment unfolded when an angelic figure appeared on the doorbell camera. Intuitively, I sensed that this celestial being had come to prepare my dad for his impending transition. Despite months of emotional struggle, I eventually accepted this divine intervention.

Simultaneously, my connection with my mirrored soul began to unravel. This detachment manifested physically in my chest, a sensation I could not easily articulate to those around me. The profound nature of my experiences prevented me from discussing them with others, as I doubted anyone would comprehend or believe my revelations. Plunging into a period of deep introspection, I entered the dark night of the soul, initiating a cathartic purging process. Months later, my mirrored soul completely detached from me, coinciding with my dad's passing.

Numbness enveloped me, and a pervasive desire to sleep dominated my days. Recollection of eating was sparse, overshadowed by a flood of spiritual downloads and personal divine interventions. In the wake of losing both my dad and the connection with my mirrored soul, a kundalini awakening ensued. Sensations of heat surged up my spine and throughout my body, marking a transformative phase following the profound experiences of death and love. This awakening also heightened my perceptions, granting me increased clarity in dreams, visions, and an unintentional development of clairaudience.

I received numerous messages from the spirit realm during this period, all while purging everything that no longer served my highest good. I had started astral traveling in my sleep—something I believe I had done previously but now could recall vividly. Those close to me, including ancestors whom I sensed but couldn't recognize from my dreams, provided comfort and guidance throughout this transformative process. I was certain that spirit was aiding me, especially as my departed loved ones left messages for me to decipher. Witnessing them frequently in my dreams made accepting death less challenging than it had been in the past.

My grandmother appeared most frequently in my dreams, leading me to believe she serves as our guardian. While my grandfather occupies a higher spiritual realm, when they both manifest together in my dreams, a rare occurrence, I recognize it as an indication of something crucial I must address. Seeking guidance, I implored the spirit to reveal my pre-incarnated self and experienced a powerful vision that stirred me awake, feeling the fire in my chest. In this dream, I stood alone, using the force of fire to eliminate threats to others' safety and championing what was just. There were only two instances when I dreamt of being an angel, and I recall them with precision.

The first instance was when I was in the process of ending my marriage. In a dream, my ex-husband handed me wings, accompanied by another figure who seemed to be involved with the spiritual laws of the land. As I walked away, I physically felt a shock in my back, an experience I firmly believe marked the beginning of my mirrored soul journey.

According to spiritual guidance, my ex-husband in this lifetime was my identical twin sibling in past lives. I was considered the more responsible one, but he wouldn't heed my advice, a dynamic typical of siblings. In this current life, the message was clear – he needed to gain independence, and I, in turn, had to prioritize self-care, having self-sacrificed in previous lifetimes. The realization shed light on why we deeply cared for each other's well-being, even though a romantic connection wouldn't work for us.

Walking away from the marriage turned out to be a crucial step. It allowed him to achieve independence and take charge of his life, and I, in turn, began to prioritize my own needs. Eventually, we both encountered our mirrored souls, individuals we had unknowingly prepared each other for during our time together. While our marriage didn't succeed, the true assignment unfolded, providing valuable life lessons for both of us.

Our connection is often misunderstood by others, and some may even envy it. However, we've maintained a friendship because we understood that the essence of our bond lay in comprehending the assignment rather than dwelling on what transpired and why.

Reflecting on it now, our relationship was unique compared to most couples. We not only shared a marriage but also worked together for a considerable period. Outsiders who didn't know us personally often referred to us as twins. At the time, I didn't grasp the comparison, but I do now. Our interactions were more akin to siblings than romantic partners, a fact that became apparent even to some of my coworkers. There were moments when our connection raised questions among his relatives too, as some thought we resembled each other or others in the family. In hindsight, these may have been subtle signs that we failed to recognize back then, but their meaning is clear to me now.

We eventually surrendered to the circumstances, moved on, and established a successful co-parenting relationship. In a subsequent dream, I found myself as an angel engaged in a battle during a distant era, possibly coinciding with the extinction of dinosaurs. Only angels populated this dream, and my role was evidently one of protection. This insight suggests that safeguarding is likely my earthly assignment, a significant responsibility given the substantial protection I sense around me.

I observe numerous synchronicities and symbolic representations, such as owls and cats appearing consistently, along with birds flying unusually low toward me. Due to my heightened level of consciousness, I perceive and feel everything, including the pain and anxiety of others. The power of my words has intensified, influencing people more profoundly, and I've become acutely aware of the need for caution in my speech, especially when the veil between realms is thin. Some individuals may possess a dormant gift of words, unaware of its existence, yet it can manifest itself unexpectedly.

There was a pivotal moment in my journey, a moment of true recognition that I was on a significant path. It occurred when I was at home on a Tuesday, and God spoke, instructing me to let Pastor Linda lay hands on me that coming Sunday. I responded with a hesitant "okay." Surprisingly, on Thursday, while at work, God repeated the same directive. I agreed once more, realizing that there was no escaping this divine instruction, especially since it had been reiterated. I understood that God probably foresaw my potential excuses and ensured that I would comply. Thus, I had to be obedient.

On the appointed Sunday, Pastor Linda didn't preach, but after Bishop delivered the sermon, she began laying hands on people. I had never experienced such a gesture before and was incredibly nervous. However, her words stayed with me. She remarked, "Your light is so bright. Let it shine, and come out of the darkness." Although I didn't fully grasp the meaning at the time, it later served as confirmation to something God had already revealed to me. The realization didn't fully settle in until God jogged my memory about my childhood dreams and statements.

During our time living near the airport as children, every time I saw a plane, I would enthusiastically declare, "I am going to ride one of those first chance I get!" I also expressed my desire to be famous and to sing because singing brought me immense joy. These were dreams I had pushed to the background due to witnessing the public struggles of famous individuals and the scrutiny of their personal lives. Additionally, the occasional plane crashes I observed on the news discouraged my desire to fly. As life progressed and I took on multiple jobs, I found myself singing less frequently and struggling to recall lyrics.

Upon reflecting on the broader perspective, I came to the realization that fear, instigated by the devil, had hindered my progress in pursuing those dreams. I had restrained myself due to persistent "what ifs," but that is no longer the case. Yes, there are numerous uncertainties, but have we ever contemplated the positive outcomes? What if this endeavor leads to significant success, contributes to building a lasting legacy for myself and my family, grants financial independence, or even plays a role in saving the world? These are the only "what ifs" I am willing to entertain this time.

Like Martin Luther King, I too have a dream—a dream that as individuals, we undertake the necessary self-work to grow and evolve spiritually. I envision a collective understanding of our purpose and the important lessons we can conquer. Let us provide our lives with the nourishment required for proper growth, releasing trivial thoughts and embracing spiritual maturity. Instead of fixating on others' flaws, let us focus on our own. Acknowledge that everyone has imperfections, and rather than attempting to change them, permit change to occur organically if they desire it. We can guide others, presenting them with opportunities, but ultimately, the choice lies within their free will. Each person has their unique path to tread, and we cannot traverse both theirs and ours.

In my pursuit of additional income, I explored various endeavors, but I chose to become a life insurance agent because my true aspiration was always to help people.

Upon examining my birth chart, I discovered that my life path number is nine, coincidentally matching the day I was born. Life path nines are recognized as humanitarians, consistently driven to offer assistance and be of service—a characterization that resonates deeply with who I am. While I had always harbored a desire to help people, I came to the realization that pursuing a career as a life insurance agent wasn't aligned with my true calling.

A spiritual prompting whispered in my ear, affirming that this path was not what was intended for me. Moreover, working as an agent at that time felt somewhat coercive and manipulative. I was aware of what was beneficial for the clients, and they were cognizant as well. However, not all were in a stable financial position to acquire insurance, and I preferred individuals expressing their readiness to protect their lives and secure their families rather than coercing them into a decision they acknowledged but were not presently equipped to undertake—likely only for a brief period if pressured.

Consequently, I opted to contribute to the well-being of others in a different capacity. While assisting in life insurance inherently aids others, I sensed that my true passion lay elsewhere. Teaching and helping people emerged as my genuine interests, a realization cultivated through various job experiences. Throughout my diverse employment history, I assumed the role of a trainer in every position. This revelation led me to pursue certification as a life and relationship coach. My inclination is to guide individuals in achieving their goals, whether substantial or modest—be it devising savings plans, preparing for retirement, organizing vacations, or enhancing communication skills.

I felt compelled to embark on this path because, in the course of my work, I encountered various personalities that struggled with understanding their health insurance plans, grasping the value of money, prioritizing tasks, and effectively communicating. Observing this, I recognized an opportunity to provide structure for some individuals and educate others who were unaware of resources available to assist them in times of need. Excelling at aiding people in these aspects and finding fulfillment even without monetary compensation, I pondered, "Why not make it a career?"

Thus, it has become my new journey, alongside the one with my mirrored soul.

In a previous mention, I spoke of recognizing my mirrored soul. However, in this lifetime, there was one other person from a past job whom I also recognized. I believe she recognized me as well because, as she entered as a new associate I needed to train, we simultaneously exclaimed, "I know you." Despite a significant age gap, our souls seemed closely aligned. During and after the training, we engaged in hours of conversation. I distinctly recall a profound discussion about her son and her apprehension about him joining the military. She recounted her efforts to dissuade him, and I offered the perspective that she needed to let him embark on his own journey, just as she had. We raise our children to become self-sufficient adults, capable of independence, and despite her resistance to change, I hoped she would accept this inevitable transition.

I hold a deep affection for her, and I sincerely hope that wherever she is now, she is leading her best life. She might have been among the first individuals I informed about my decision to leave the job we were both currently engaged in, sharing the news over dinner. The revelation brought her to tears because we had developed a strong bond as kindred spirits. While she didn't take the news well, she accepted it without a choice.

Many of my coworkers, whom I had recently trained, expressed reluctance to continue working there if I were to leave, and I believe a few of them departed shortly after my departure. One coworker, in particular, mentioned that the aspect she would miss the most was my assistance during open enrollment and the patience I exhibited while doing so.

Reflecting on my journey, I now recognize several instances when messages from the spirit eluded me initially. A male coworker, who had dubbed me "movie star" for years without knowing my name, insisted that I looked like a star. He would often say, "Girl, you are a star, and you don't even know it," countless times before actually learning my name, likely spanning over years.

While the journey presented numerous challenges, the most arduous aspect was witnessing those close to me confront adversity. In certain situations, the spirit had to remind me multiple times to stay out of certain matters. I was told, "They need to go through adversity as you did to grow and learn."

They will never grasp the lesson or learn it if you consistently stand in their way. Consequently, I allow God to orchestrate what must unfold; in truth, I have no choice in the matter. However, I must come to terms with the understanding that whatever challenges they encounter are ultimately for their highest good. Although I cannot bring myself to witness their struggles, I choose to pray for a soft landing.

It has been crucial for me to acknowledge the dual nature of this world. Embracing both the good and the bad is a necessary aspect of navigating life. Accepting that things may not always go as planned and recognizing our imperfections are essential components of our existence. We are here to ascend, attain enlightenment, and transcend. As part of this journey, I've learned the importance of distancing myself from material possessions that many hold dear. While possessions can be beneficial, they do not define who I am.

I have resolved not to purchase items from individuals on the street, particularly if the value of the possession surpasses the time they spent preparing for the day. As a business owner myself, I cannot justify supporting the acquisition of stolen goods, as doing so only perpetuates such behavior. I genuinely wish that those who engage in theft would redirect their time and effort towards personal growth, investing in themselves, and building their own legacy. While everyone progresses at different rates, I can only hope that this transformation occurs sooner rather than later.

During this journey, I slept extensively, and within my dreams, I found myself in a profound state. I recall a particular instance when I slept for over eight hours, and throughout this time, all I could hear was the phrase "white lotus flower," against a black backdrop. Intrigued, upon awakening, I sought to understand the significance of a white lotus flower, as it was the sole theme resonating in my dreams. It symbolizes awakening, embodying a spiritually pure mental state, and is associated with peace. Remarkably, it has the ability to thrive in murky waters while maintaining its purity, symbolizing rebirth—a parallel to my Scorpio birth sun sign.

During my prolonged sleep, I mistakenly felt as though I were on the brink of death, considering that those undergoing transitions often cease regular activities and eating habits. It dawned on me later that I was undergoing a rebirth, akin to a butterfly transforming just before its emergence.

Along this transformative path, certain individuals have left lasting impressions, with one male coworker standing out prominently. On his final working day, which closely preceded my own departure, he expressed that I possessed one of the most innovative minds he had encountered. Such affirmations echoed sentiments expressed by my late father and spirit, affirming that I am indeed a smart individual.

In my current job, which I adore for its diverse community and the flexibility I specifically requested from the spiritual realm, I occasionally sense a misalignment. Despite the friendly and respectful nature of those around me, there exists a one-dimensional thinking that prevails. However, this feeling shifted upon meeting someone I refer to as "baby girl."

I was on autopilot for a considerable period before getting to know any of my coworkers. It seemed as though time stood still until the day we were assigned to the same station. Despite her youth, she exuded an adult demeanor, likely influenced by our midnight work hours. She frequently spoke about school, mentioning lengthy hours spent there. When she disclosed leaving work for a seven-hour school session, I inquired about the kind of school that required such extended classes and the subjects she was taking.

To my surprise, she revealed she attended my high school and was still a student there. The protective instinct within me surfaced, and I entered prayer and protection mode, recognizing the challenges she faced. It was astonishing that she managed to work under those circumstances, a feat I attributed to the grace of God. On our first day working together, we engaged in conversation and laughter throughout the night—a rarity for me since the separation from my mirrored soul years ago.

As our connection deepened over time, I eventually revealed my age, as she seemed to perceive us as close in age, perhaps in soul years. It turned out she was younger than my daughter, yet she continued to inquire about "the baby" as if she were older than my daughter. When I shared my age, there was a brief pause before she humorously remarked, "black don't crack, do it," and we both shared a laugh. Over time, our bond strengthened, and I felt at ease enough to invite her to join me for Easter service at church.

We sat in the car after the service, engaged in conversation. During our talk, I shared with her the revelation that I have a twin soul, and she inquired about its meaning. I explained that a twin soul is someone with similar characteristics to mine, a distinct individual with whom I share an exact spiritual DNA. This person comprehends me on a profound level, surpassing anyone else. I expressed that, mentally, I couldn't be with anyone else because I was aware of the unique connection and potential we shared. This was a sentiment I had never disclosed to anyone but her, solidifying our connection as kindred spirits. Spirit had conveyed to me that I would encounter individuals from my soul family.

I confided in her about my ongoing search for someone who could match up to my twin soul, emphasizing that we still had unfinished business. Although Spirit had indicated that our separation was intentional, with the assurance of a reunion at an unspecified time, I knew it would occur when both of us were ready. This separation served a purpose, preventing us from jeopardizing a relationship that, in reality, was not damaged but required internal work to bring forth joy. Despite being physically separated, we maintained constant telepathic communication.

There were instances when I sensed his emotional distress, leading me to silently question, "Who used you?" internally. Yet, recognizing my inability to see the events unfold, I would release the inquiry. Upon our eventual reunion, he validated everything I had already intuited, and what's even more astonishing is that, even during our time apart, we consistently found ourselves engaged in similar types of work. Our shared traumas further highlighted the synchronicity between us.

Many may wonder about the connection between my mirrored soul journey and my spirituality. Mirrored Souls represent a divine connection and serve as a catalyst for the transformative changes we must undergo within ourselves. They reveal our shadow side; the aspect we might wish to ignore but acknowledge its existence. In my case, this connection guided me to the path I was destined to tread, fostering a more profound relationship with Spirit. Through my individual spiritual journey, I successfully interlinked the dots of my various life experiences—whether in the professional realm, friendships, or intimate relationships. This intricate web of connections has played a pivotal role in bringing me to the present point in my life.

Chapter Ten - The Astrology of My Birth Chart

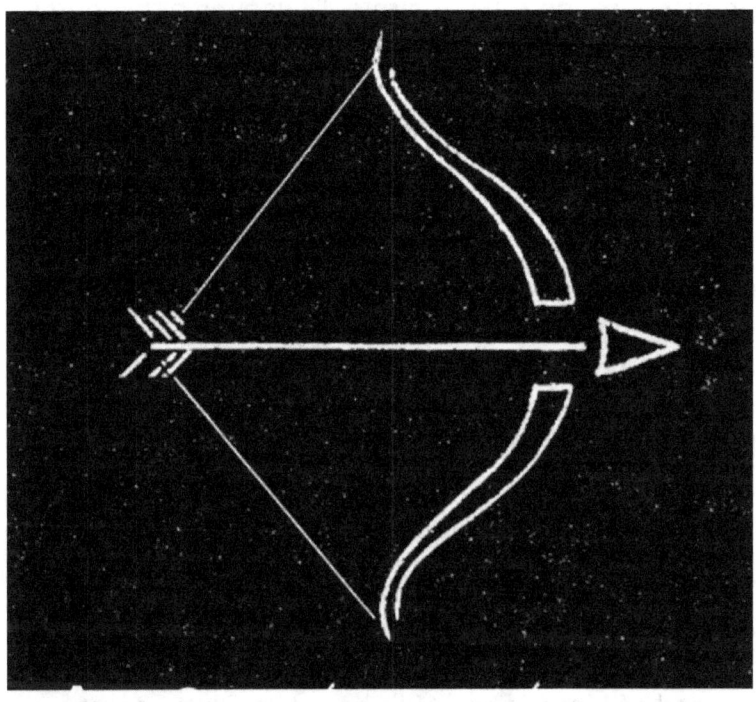

I cannot overlook the significant role that astrology has played in my spiritual journey. While I won't delve too deeply, I've always been captivated by astrology—drawn to it, to be precise. Upon researching my birth chart, I discovered enlightening details that provided insight into the challenges I would face in this lifetime and how I could navigate through them. It unveiled aspects of my past experiences with individuals who have crossed my path. What began as a mere exploration of my birth chart turned out to be a profound revelation, akin to a life navigation tool, much like the navigation systems on our phones.

For those not well-versed in astrology, I can attempt to elucidate it based on my understanding, emphasizing that it goes beyond merely reading a horoscope to predict one's day. To illustrate, I'll use my birth chart as an example. As a Sagittarius rising, Mercury, Mars, and Neptune form my 1st house (rising sign), representing the way the world perceives me. In my 11th house, I have a Scorpio Sun, Venus, and Uranus, with the Sun symbolizing my soul. Additionally, the South Node and Moon in Pisces represent my emotions. While people often pass judgments based on sun signs, the reality is that many of us might resonate more with our rising signs—the first house of self. Without knowledge of one's birthplace and time of birth, this crucial aspect may remain unknown. Despite being a Scorpio, inclined towards introspection, the strong influence of Sagittarius in my chart prevents me from dwelling in that inner space for too long.

At times, I find myself grappling with indecision, often attributing it to specific astrological placements. I am mindful of Libra in my 10th house in Pluto, as well as Virgo in Saturn and North Node. According to what I've read, individuals on a spiritual journey tend to focus on their North Node, representing an area where they have overcome challenges. Virgo, associated with money, family, and foundation, seems to reflect aspects I may not have given much importance to in previous lifetimes. Not that I disregarded them entirely, but my focus likely leaned more towards spirituality, with material possessions holding minimal sway then and now. To me, material things are replaceable and insurable, unlike life itself, which is more valuable.

Understanding these placements prompted me to explore favorable and less favorable times for taking risks. In my perspective, the movement of planets acts as a cosmic timekeeper, and decoding their significance in my birth chart empowers me to make more informed decisions. During void periods, I practice stillness, and when in retrograde, I exercise caution before committing to significant decisions. I limit communication during retrograde phases, recognizing that misunderstandings and petty disagreements tend to escalate during such times.

With this knowledge, I've cultivated a sense of peace amid the happenings around me, as I comprehend the underlying reasons behind events. This aspect has become a pivotal part of my spiritual journey, offering tranquility through the awareness of why certain occurrences unfold when they do.

I cannot overlook the significance of the planet Jupiter in my birth chart, symbolizing expansion and luck. It is positioned in the zodiac placements of Leo, which represents the Sun. The incredible luck I have experienced is likely attributed to the configuration of my birth chart. Despite the inevitable challenges we all face, there is a unique blessing in being spiritually prepared months, and at times, even years ahead of time.

While I have encountered numerous challenges, the ability to navigate and overcome them was facilitated by pre-existing plans. This foresight lessened the impact of the falls, making the journey feel less arduous.

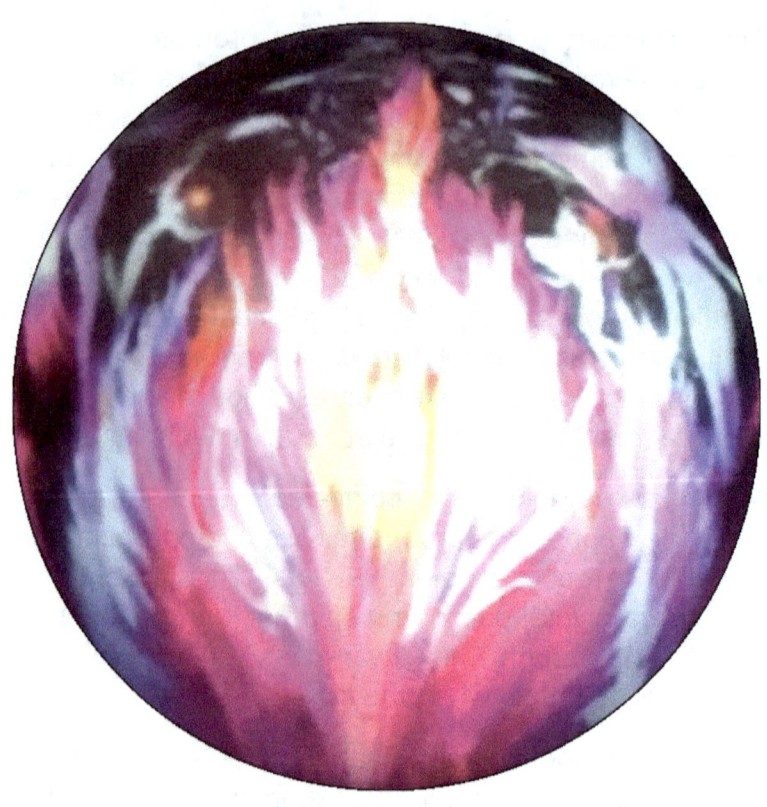

I am the light, a pure light, eliminating all negative energy, replacing with positive, for a more peaceful and sustainable life.

www.ingramcontent.com/pod-product-compliance
Lightning Source LLC
Chambersburg PA
CBHW070944120626
46546CB00004B/1553